The

Tora Karate

Instructor's Manual

Developed by Sensei Jeff Waters, 5th Dan

We are the sum of our experiences. I was very fortunate to be gifted with inspirational teachers whose enthusiasm was so profound that I still find myself drawing on their examples when I teach.
I hope that those who chose to teach find as much fulfilment and sense of purpose in it as I have.
Thank you to all who encouraged me and thank you to the students and parents who posed for the photos.

Photo treatments by Tim Maloney

Edited by Barry Connors, Windsor, Ontario

Published by Barry B. Connors
ISBN:0994094523
ISBN-13:978-0-9940945-2-0

Tora Karate Instructor's Manual

Welcome to the rewarding world of Karate instruction! This manual is designed to provide you with the foundation to become a great instructor. The skills you will develop will carry you throughout your life and aid you in anything else you wish to accomplish.

Teaching is one of the few acts that reward both the student and the instructor. The student improves by learning techniques and methods and the instructor's base of knowledge widens and deepens with every class. It is no secret at Tora that the very best martial artists are also instructors. This has always been the case throughout the history of the club. Let's start there: the history of Tora.

The Tora Karate Club was established in Quebec in 1981 by Barry Connors. Prior to that Sensei Connors and his family lived in Ontario and were part of Tora Martial Arts under Sensei Howell. Sensei Connors was offered a great opportunity to work in Montreal and moved his family there. Once settled in, Sensei Connors started looking for Wado clubs in Montreal as he was a brown belt at the time. He tried a few but thought they were missing something. He had been very fortunate when he was in Ontario in that he had Sensei Howell as an instructor. Sensei Howell was a very patient instructor and truly put his heart into making his students the best that they could be. That generosity of self was the missing piece that Sensei Connors was searching for. When he visited one club, the instructor felt he had to hurt Sensei Connors to prove his position. That was enough. Disappointed, Sensei Connors was at a loss for what to do. He had put a lot of time and effort into his

art, along with his children, and did not look forward to maybe changing arts or stopping all together. Sensei Connors late wife, Mary, took it upon herself to contact Sensei Howell and tell him about the experience. This led to Sensei Howell suggesting that Sensei Connors start his own club with his support. Mary proceeded to search for local available sites and put the wheels in motion unbeknownst to Sensei Connors. Flyers were posted around stores and one poster ended up in Lindsay Place High School, where Michael, their oldest son was attending. This is where I came in. I saw the flyer and called up. I was fourteen at the time and really didn't catch on to why there was such an enthusiastic response from them! The time arrived for my first class and when I found the school, I was ushered in by a very excited Michael and Tammie, their daughter who was also a karate student. I looked around but there was no instructor. Then I heard a surprised voice asking, "What is this?" and there stood a man with a huge smile and a look of shock on his face. "It's your karate club!", was the response from Mary, Michael and Tammie. I have studied under Sensei Connors since that time. I was very fortunate throughout the years to be able to have met Sensei Howell and see what inspired that teaching from the heart that made Tora so special. Since 1981, I have had the
opportunity to speak with many martial artists from a variety of styles and one truth keeps surfacing; a good instructor can make all the difference and help the art come alive for a student. When I meet past Tora students, it is truly as if I am meeting family. Tora has taught well over 2500 students since 1981, so that is one big family!

Tora Karate Instructor's Manual Index

1) Why should I become an instructor?
2) I don't plan on opening a karate school. Why should I learn to teach?
3) I'm only a lower rank and not a black belt. How can I teach at this level?
4) I don't know if my technique is good enough to be teaching someone else. Should I really be teaching?
5) I don't feel like a teacher, just a student.
6) What is the difference between teaching Juniors and Adults?
7) What if I forget a technique in front of the students?
8) I'm a teenager. I feel kind of weird teaching someone twice my age.
9) Why is teaching a requirement for ranking at Tora?
10) My Juniors aren't listening. What do I do?
11) How do I teach a brand new student?
12) OK, I've tried the praise and attention, but my junior is still misbehaving.
13) I don't want to be known as the mean instructor. Can't I just have fun with the kids?
14) This is getting ridiculous! The student is still not behaving after all the push-ups. Now what?
15) I'm explaining the movements but the students don't seem to be getting it. What can I do?
16) I have a particularly bright or gifted student in front of me that seems to know a technique better than I do. What should I do with him/her?
17) I have a student who thinks they are really gifted and already know the techniques. How to do I get that student to focus?
18) Oh oh, my student just injured him/herself. What do I do?
19) My student is telling me that they were taught the technique differently by another instructor and they are asking, "which is the right way?"
20) I'm OK with teaching a few students at a time but teaching the whole class is a different story, isn't it?
21) I made it through the warm-up, now everyone is wondering what's next?

Everyone has heard the phrase, " It takes a village to raise a child", and in my 35 years of Karate, I have had the privilege to both witness the truth of these words, and to be a part of the process.

This book was written as a manual for the instructors in my club, but if the truth be told, the methodology found within could be applied to most instructional endeavours. Personally, these tools helped me to become a better parent, a better teacher, and even a better employee. Of course without the students to give me the opportunity to explore the myriad combinations of behaviours, not much could be learned. Karate is more than punches and kicks, it is a way of life and this manual is just one more example of how it can enrich ones life.

Jeff Waters is the owner operator of Tora Karate Club Quebec Inc., and holds a 5th dan in a traditional Japanese karate style called Wado. He teaches at his clubs and as a guest at others. He also taught karate as an extra-curricular program in many elementary schools. Jeff is also a pilot and gliding instructor at the Gatineau Gliding club in Ontario.

1) Why should I become an instructor?

Every puzzle has a prize. Everyone has taught something at one point in their life. This could be something as simple as teaching a younger sibling how to walk, colour, dress, or teaching a friend a neat thing that you alone know how to do. Without realizing it, when you taught that skill, you re-taught it to yourself; organizing it in your mind with greater clarity than before. Karate is no different. Every time you teach a particular subject, your knowledge grows in that field. You will be asked questions from such different points of view that you would have never thought of that you will be forced to expand your own understanding. This is your prize. The good part is that this is an endless fountain where the more you teach, the more you learn. As mentioned earlier, take a look at fellow karateka or martial artists and you find that ones with the sharpest technique and broadest base of knowledge are the ones who teach.

2) I don't plan on opening a karate school. Why should I learn to teach?

Knowledge and experience are transferable. By learning teaching skills here you will be able to apply them anywhere. I know it works as I have been asked to instruct in other activities like work or at my gliding club. Most of what I have learned about being a good parent has been discovered by teaching juniors and studying their responses to teaching. Juniors are young people who are very honest with their feelings and reactions. If you are able to get your point across to them, you will be able to do so in other environments. You will start to recognize similar responses and reactions in general and this will help you in all aspects of life. As I rose up in my company into positions with more responsibility, my ability to understand the behaviour of people and their reactions was a valuable asset. I could look beyond words of frustration and be able to get to the root of a problem and solve it.

3) I'm only a lower rank and not a black belt. How can I teach at this level?

I'm going to let you in on a little secret. Nobody instantly becomes an expert in something when a rank or a title is bestowed on him. You might hear things like, "Wow! She got promoted to that new management position. Is she ever lucky!" A really bright university professor, Richard Donovan, said there is no such thing as luck. Planning, preparation, and hard work + opportunity = LUCK. If you constantly work and prepare yourself diligently, you will be in the right place and time when opportunity knocks on your door. It is the same with instruction. You start learning to instruct by teaching the ranks that you just came from. You reinforce everything you learned to get to where you are and the neat part is that you will hardly notice the amount of review you are doing. If you are or end up being a professional like a Doctor, Engineer, Accountant, Pilot or otherwise, part of maintaining your title will be devoted to constant review. It is a fact of life. The professionals that teach their craft always end up being current and are generally the best in their field.

Teaching compels you to review and reorganize what you know. In some ways, when you teach the ranks just below you, the students may identify with you because you just came from where they are and you know first hand the issues they are trying to overcome. This is why higher ranks will value your effort and opinion because you are closest to knowing what those students are going through. In business, there is a general rule called the three-meter rule, which loosely states that the person to best solve a particular problem will probably be within three meters of the problem. Imagine you are building a car in an assembly line. There is a problem with the way a part goes together. An engineer in another building or city has done a great deal of thinking on how to put the part together but may have missed something. You happen to see one minor detail that could be changed to make the assembly work. You have the experience of putting that part together hundreds of times. You become the problem solver.

4) I don't know if my technique is good enough to be teaching someone else. Should I really be teaching?

I'm going to let you in on another secret. I was not Sensei Connors best student. As a matter of fact, I was one of the worst and least coordinated. There were others that picked up techniques twice or three times as quickly as I did, at first. How did Sensei Connors help me? He asked me to teach the very technique that I was having trouble with. How did I feel about that? At first I hated it. Nobody likes to have to demonstrate their weakness to someone else. Ask people who are shy about crowds if they like to do speeches. You know the answer. Gradually my technique improved because I had to teach it. This forced me to review it and practice it. I had to really analyze every part of that technique from top to bottom. In the end, the student got good at it and so did I. Be honest with yourself and your student and do not be shy to say that you are still trying to improve your own technique.

5) I don't feel like a teacher, I feel like a student.

I feel like a student too. One of the scariest two words to come out of a students mouth is "I know". It is best to always think of yourself as a student. That doesn't mean you will not be a good teacher, it means you have potential to be a great teacher. A great teacher is always in a state of learning; always looking for how to get their students to improve. Sensei Connors always said that your students will push you up. This is true. The more you give to your students, the more you will learn.

I had another great teacher, Bob Mercer, who was a Captain flying 747s for Air Canada. Imagine how good he had to be to have the responsibility of 500 lives on his plane. He was my gliding instructor. One time he asked to borrow my basic flying textbook. I was so surprised that I had to ask what he needed it for. He told me that he had heard that the code for how weather was reported was going to change and he wanted to be up to date. Learning never stops no matter how high in rank you get or how accomplished you are. Never be afraid to be a student.

6) What is the difference between teaching Juniors and Adults?

Teaching each group has different challenges and benefits. Adults have been learning for a while by now and will be able to pick up techniques sooner. They may have more resolve to keep trying until they get it and will not need as much motivation from you...up to a point. One of the challenges of teaching an adult is that they have learned to interpret. If you are not extremely clear with your instruction, your adult student may still get the idea. On the negative side, even if you are giving clear instruction, your adult student may interpret and think you mean something else. Junior students will be more literal. By that I mean that if you ask for a particular movement, you will probably get it exactly as you describe it or demonstrate it. A Junior will not think "oh, I think he/she wants me to do this". So if a Junior does exactly what he is shown, guess what? They will copy every mistake that you make too. Is this a bad thing? No, because they are acting like a mirror to yourself, you will correct what you see and in turn you will correct and improve yourself. What kind of challenges can you expect teaching an adult? As I mentioned before, adults are motivated and they are used to learning things pretty quickly.

Karate is not a quickly learned art. At times they will be frustrated at their progress or they may compare themselves to other students. They can be very hard on themselves and your task as an instructor will be to try to encourage them to keep on trying. One of the best things you can do is be open and honest with your own experience and try and remember how frustrating it was when you tried to learn your first kata.

7) What if I forget a technique in front of the students?

Welcome to my world. Learning Karate is like learning to juggle balls. You start out with one or two and they are easy to keep track of and you can add a third. Get up to black belt and now you are trying to keep twenty or more balls in the air at one time. Once in a while a ball might fall down. What to do? Smile, pick it up and start juggling again. Forgetting a technique in front of a student is going to happen. The more you teach, the more rarely this will happen but it will happen. What is the best response? Tell them the truth. Tell them that you want to teach them the right technique and that you will find out. If you can't get an answer from an instructor right away, make very sure that when you do get the answer you find the students you were teaching afterwards and tell them what you found out. Think about it; you will look like an instructor that truly cares about their student's progress. They will appreciate your effort. I always did when someone found out for me. You never look bad when you have your heart in the right place and want your student to succeed. Be true to your word though. If you say you are going to find out, do it.

8) I'm a teenager. I feel kind of weird teaching someone twice my age.

This is normal. You are probably someone who respects people older than you and so far older people have always known more than you in just about everything. This is a great opportunity for you. You have a chance to make a very good impression and learn about your own abilities. Remember that in our club, the thing that really matters is your rank and your character. Your rank will help at first, as it will be obvious that you know what you are doing or you wouldn't have received it. Your character will help in that even though you are a higher rank, you will show respect for the older person. You won't have to give push-ups to an older person nor should you.

If you actually encounter a problem where you are in a situation where you would normally give push-ups to a junior, it is time to bow to your student and seek a black belt. Since I have started in Tora, I have rarely, if ever, seen a case where an adult was not respectful to a younger person of higher rank who was teaching. Remember, you should be returning the respect you receive in equal or greater quantities. An adult will be going through an adjustment too as in their world it is rare that a person nearly half their age is teaching them. As long as you do your best to make them the best student you can, you will both come out winning.

9) Why is teaching a requirement for ranking at Tora?

Make no mistake. You are learning a lethal martial art. We don't play with our karate, we don't go out seeking trophies and we don't water down our art. We have already covered some of the physical reasons you teach in that your technique improves tremendously and your understanding of the art deepens but that isn't enough. Teaching tells us a lot about your character. You may be thinking, "People can act like a good character". This is true up to a point but teaching can bring out the best and the worst in a person. Teaching will try your patience to the limit. Teaching requires commitment and responsibility. A person can only fake these things for so long and at one point they may feel the art is not for them. The more techniques you learn and the better you are able to execute them, the more you will need to be patient, kind, and understanding. You will need to be very slow to take offence and very quick to forgive. Being a teacher will help with all of this. You will also be setting the example for your students and as you go higher in rank you will feel a sense of responsibility for their development. Teaching karate will give you problem solving skills and will help you learn about yourself. Many martial art books will state the same truth: Know your enemy, know yourself. Once you know more about yourself, you will be able to understand both friend and foe.

10) My Juniors aren't listening. What do I do?

Not all Juniors begged their mom or dad to come to karate.
Some juniors might be there because it is hoped that they will
learn more focus, discipline and concentration. To this date,
Tora has never refused a student, regardless of any disability.
Some students may find karate exceedingly difficult and when a
child finds something really difficult, they can tend to drift off or
just plain wish they were somewhere else. Nothing brings a
student back to earth like hearing their name. It is very
important to learn your students name and ask the correct way
to pronounce it. After the bow, it is one of the first lessons of
respect you can give a student in that you reinforce that they are
important to you.

I'm sure you remember a time when a person in authority forgot
your name and how it made you feel. Use positive words of
encouragement. Everyone likes attention. If you have a junior
that is doing something silly, he is probably after attention. For
some the need is so strong that they don't really care what kind
of attention they get. This will manifest iteself in the form of
acting in ways that make the other juniors laugh to, in rare cases,
using hurtful words. What to do? At first, ignore the negative
behaviour. Ask the other students to look over at you. This will
remove some of the attention from the misbehaving junior.
Next, as soon as you see the tiniest improvement in behaviour or
what looks like an attempt to follow along, give lots of praise and
attention. Use words like Johnny, good job! Now you look like
you are learning some karate!

11) How do I teach a brand new student?

Try and put yourself in your new student's feet (we don't wear shoes in class 😌). It is really important to try and remember back to your first lesson. What were you feeling? What were your concerns? How overwhelmed were you? Unless the student has studied some martial art before, the entire experience will be quite foreign, starting with the fact that they were asked to take off their shoes! Nobody likes to stand out so one of the things a student will be looking for is how to fit in. I have been asked numerous times by new students if it is OK if they just hang out at the back at first. In older traditions, the highest ranking students stood in front of the instructor with the newest in the back. We do things a little differently in that we like the new student to only have to concentrate on the instructor. Although they may feel a bit on the spot, they will also not have to look at all the people that have higher ranks and more experience. They only have to work on themselves. As a student goes higher in rank, there is a sense of accomplishment as they can see where they have been; like looking back at a mountain you have climbed.

A new student will wish to fit in by learning proper protocol like how and when to bow and how to sit Seiza (Japanese style). Be aware that the older a new student is the harder they will first find that sitting position. Give them time and remember how hard it was for you. A new student may find the warm up a challenge. They will be using muscles that may have been relatively inactive for a while. Encourage them to take it easy. After a while you may be able to read a student and know if you are overdoing it. A new student will want to keep up. I have had students run out of the dojo to be sick even though they were repeatedly asked to ease up on the workout. Junior students will also find the warm-up a challenge but they will recover quite quickly. Never the less, watch them carefully and make sure they are not turning pale.

Once the warm-up is done, new students are generally given an instructor and taken aside. They will appreciate it as they will soon see how much there is to learn. Start with a review of the bow, talk to them a little as they catch their breath and then go into teaching basics. These are covered in the ranking requirements hand out. This is a key point in their training. You are the one who will set the tone of the dojo and their training. Show them your best movement and let them know that you found it tough at first. Give them breaks often at first when teaching Kibadachi. It is very easy to take your own stamina for granted when you have been studying karate for a while. You will not be able to have any positive impact on a student if you scare them away from the dojo. You may run out of things to teach but remember that in reality you only have a maximum of 20-25 minutes of technique instruction when you include the game or the burnout. Their brains are usually saturated at that point if you have been giving lots of details and encouragement and then it is time for the game or burnout. Take an interest in how your student does in the burnout. You will be able to see them as you are at least a rank behind them. At the end of the class, ask them how they feel, what they thought about the class. Advise them that it is very normal to feel sore if not the next day, then the day after a workout. Encourage them to come back. Remember that our classes are usually at night and that means that your student was at school or work all day and is giving up their evening in order to come to class. If the dojo is a fun and positive place to go, half of the battle is won.

12) OK, I've tried the praise and attention, but my junior is still misbehaving.

If your junior is now at the point where the other student's learning is suffering, the next level of correction at Tora is push-ups. The phrase is, "Ok Johnny, give me five push-ups." It is very important as they do the push-ups to tell them why they are doing them. "You are doing five push-ups because you were talking when I was explaining to the other students." Although it may be a challenge, your next act in your mind is to try and give the student a fresh page or a new chance to do well. Again, the instant you see the student trying to follow along, give lots of positive praise and tell them why they are getting it. The whole idea is to get that junior to crave good attention instead of bad (push-ups) and to be consistent. Follow through. If you give a warning and tell them that if a behaviour is repeated you will give them push-ups, you must follow through.

13) I don't want to be known as the stern instructor. Can't I just have fun with the kids?

Of course! That's one of the main attractions of Tora. We are nice people and even though we are learning a martial art, we can still have fun and continue to be really nice people with a good sense of humour. As long as your students are following along don't be afraid to give them big smiles and lots of praise. An occasional laugh is good as long as the karate lesson gets done. This again is where your mental training comes into play. You need to be able to change appearance from "Let's have fun" to "Let's train hard and not fool around" in an instant. Be prepared when you meet a new group of students. They will test your resolve. Just think back to your own school days when a substitute teacher arrived. How did the class behave? It is best at first to teach straight karate and make sure the students understand that their job is to learn and your job is to teach. If you start off as their joking friend, you will have a very difficult time bringing the group in line for instruction. Once everyone has a good understanding of the ground rules, then you can gradually introduce the fun factor. The instant things start to get silly though, ease back on the fun and get back on track.

14) This is getting ridiculous! The student is still not behaving after all the push-ups. Now what?

At this point, you are probably starting to feel frustrated or flustered. You may even begin to start feeling annoyed. These are normal reactions and now it is time for you to use some of your karate training and maintain your calm. Remember, the student's unconscious goal is still to get lots of attention. A blow-up on your part will in many ways reward his bad behaviour. Don't give in. It is now the moment for a time out. Keep your emotions in check. A good martial artist maintains mind over emotion. Use the phrase " Johnny, go stand over there and face the wall and do not move. You may have to go with him. Do not physically force him. I have never had to do that. As you walk over, quietly and calmly explain why they are being timed out. This has to be done in as few words as possible; ten or less. " Johnny, you are being timed out because you hit Jill." Take a look at the clock. The first time out should only be 30 seconds. This sounds short on paper but it is long enough. While the junior is being timed out, they cannot be allowed to lean on the wall, turn and look back at the other students or move around.

For many juniors with a good conscience, this will be plenty. At the typical age of a junior, they are well past the age of time outs. You may see red eyes or an embarrassed face. Now is the time to wipe the slate clean. At thirty seconds, ask out loud if they are ready to try karate again. Usually the answer is yes. Try to wipe your own mental slate clean and reward good behaviour right away. They need to know it is possible to still do well. Try your very best not to hang on to the frustration you may have felt when you timed the student out. If the behaviour persists, try a longer time out in fifteen-second increases. It is probably time now to seek the head instructor if you cannot teach your other students because of the junior in question. The junior now needs to know that his parent will be told about his behaviour. At Tora, I cannot recall one instance where a junior had to be asked to sit out the rest of the class but it can be a last resort and will be handled by the head instructor. Let's remember that the class isn't mandatory so almost all the juniors are there because they want to learn karate and have fun.

15) I'm explaining the movements but the students don't seem to be getting it. What can I do?

If you have ever heard the expression "Monkey see, monkey do", Karate is an activity that seems to be built around the phrase; at least at the beginner's level. If you have ever had to put anything together with instructions be it furniture, a Kinder ⓒ surprise, a puzzle, you will instantly know if it is going to be an easy task as soon as you look at the instructions. If there are lots of clear step-by-step pictures, you will probably have an easier time than cryptic text-only instructions. Give your students a beautiful picture. It is one thing to tell them what to do, but it is so much more to show them what you mean. From a very early age, humans learn by mimicking what they see.

Students will use you as the example so you may feel a little bit of pressure to give them the best example possible. This is where your own technique improves. We always want to look our best in front of others. It is human nature. Now you can put that impulse to very constructive use. Every time you move in front of your student, try and demonstrate the best technique that you can. Think of the details that you look for in your students. Now if you are thinking that you are only a certain rank and don't know all the details, don't worry too much. Explain it from the details that you do know. You will notice that you are almost never given students of an equal or higher rank than yourself so you will either have a better understanding of the movements or more time on the floor. Once you give the best demonstration that you can and the students have done the movement with you several times, come out of your stance and observe each student while keeping up your count.

The students will need the repetition to really get the movement into their subconscious so don't be shy to continue. As you study your student's movements, be generous with positive comments when you see someone doing what you consider to be good movement. Watch the reaction from the other students as you comment and you probably see them pick up on what you are saying and their movement will also improve. Remember to use words that tell them why they are getting praised, for example, " That stance is really looking good. I can see that you understand that the front knee needs to be bent so you can see your big and your second toe." Vary your comments based on what you see. Vary the length of your comments. Sometimes all that is required is a very short positive comment. Be very quick to demonstrate your movement again so the students are working from a clear and recent picture. In an interview, Cus D'Amato, Mike Tyson's first boxing coach recalls that to get Mike to improve in something, he would praise him for the act before he had done it. This had the effect of Mike striving to live up to the praise that had been given. In small doses with your students, this may be effective too.

16) I have a particularly bright or gifted student in front of me that seems to know a technique better than I do. What should I do with him/her?

There are always going to be those students that just seem to "get it" with very little effort and you may feel at a loss for what to do with them when they are in a group of the same rank you are teaching. Turn the obstacle into an opportunity. If the student truly has that good a technique, use them up front to demonstrate alongside you. If you are doing a kata as a group, put that bright student at the back so when you are reversing along the pattern, they can be the example. You generally won't have too much trouble with the really gifted students as they will still want to excel and if you watch them long enough, you can still find elements to improve upon. The higher the student goes in rank the more likely it will be that you may be looking two students of equal rank and yet different levels of knowledge. It takes quite a while to obtain a higher rank and one student may have just arrived at that level while the other is just on the way to the next. Within the group you are teaching, you may also ask that student who may be going in rank soon to work one-on-one with the student that just arrived at that rank. This will leave you with a more generalized group.

Challenge that gifted student with as much detail to a technique as they can handle and be careful that they do not fall to the wayside. This can happen quite easily since they can blend in easily with the other students in a group setting; it is easy for them to do what you ask. When you give that little extra tweak to the gifted student and they learn to apply it well, they will inspire the ranks beside and below them. It is one think to watch a black belt perform a crisp technique and a student may say to themselves, "Well sure they can do that, they're a black belt". It is another thing when they see a rank close to their own doing something equally impressive because it becomes something more readily attainable. The more students you have walking around with, "I think I do that" in their minds, the better your class will be. While it may be difficult to your sense of fairness, accept the fact that occasionally, you may have to rank that gifted student sooner than the others, as long as they are contributing to the group through teaching. Bear in mind that it is your decision, not the parents, and not the students themselves. Even gifted students will reach plateaus and if they used to ranking quickly, they will feel the lag more strongly than the average student that just consistently keeps at it.

17) I have a student who thinks they are really gifted and already know the techniques. How to do I get that student to focus?

Some students are very ambitious and tend to look at karate as a giant buffet laid out in front of them. They can't wait to sample everything so they tend to really try hard to pick up as many techniques as they can as quickly as they can. Here is where that old expression ' Jack of all trades, master of none' may come into play. Everyone at karate needs to learn or overcome something. This student may need to learn patience. There is nothing wrong with being ambitious, most karateka tend to be the type of person to not give up on anything, but finding balance in anything is always important. With this type of student, you will want to try and bring out the desire to polish their techniques further before reaching for the next cool thing. Take a good hard look at their technique and see what they could improve. There may be a temptation to 'knock them down a peg or two', meaning telling them they aren't as good as they think they are but if you take a position like that early in the game, your student may put up a mental barrier that will keep you from really helping them. You may be able to get them on side by first recognizing their achievement.

Remember that this student has many of the qualities that you would want in a student; eagerness to learn, energy, enthusiasm and they will more than likely inspire this in others if you can bring them into focus. Tell your student that you are impressed that they have come.along very quickly and learned a lot for their rank. You may use the black belts as an example and explain how they are still working on the very first kata to try and get it right. It takes time to build a good foundation that will last. Depending on the student's age, there are many examples or analogies you could use. For a younger student, you may want to use building a tower of Lego© as an example. If they try and just put block on top of block, their tower will fall down after just a little. If they make the bottom really wide, their tower can keep on growing but it may take a little more time to build the tower. In older students you could use the example of building a house in that you need to make a good, solid foundation or basement first or the house will fall no matter how pretty it looks above ground. Once you have the student on your side, go up through the techniques from the basics and gently suggest areas to improve.

18) Uh oh, my student just injured him/herself. What do I do?

Injuries, thankfully, are pretty rare at Tora. We are a non-contact club and as such we don't put students in harm's way in a confrontational manner. However, occasionally a student may try a bit too hard to master a technique and may strain a muscle or feel a little sick. The universal sign a student will give in our club and in many others is to go down on one knee. It serves at least two immediate purposes. In a group of students, one at a much lower height is easy to spot. As well, if a student is close to fainting, lowering the body will momentarily increase the blood pressure and the student may have a little less far to fall. If the student has sprained a joint or muscle, the student should be asked/told to stop the exercise and go to the side. If your student protests, explain that it is very important to not try to keep on working or pushing through an injury. Explain that there is no shame whatsoever in finding or recognizing one's limits. The student also needs to know that by continuing to try and train with an injury will actually slow down their progress. It is better to let the injury heal. If your student gets injured, they become your immediate priority. Ask another student to take the count of the current exercise or send the students to another instructor while you deal with your injured student. You should ask for help from your sensei. Now is not the time to be polite. Do not feel shy to call out in a clear voice that you would like some help.

Do not let your injured student walk away or leave the dojo without you or your sensei knowing.

Many students may feel embarrassed at feeling sick or faint and it is a common thing for these people to walk away. Do not allow this or follow them if you have to, as they should not be left alone. Tora has first aid responders that are members of the club and they will help you. You may wish to take part in a first aid/CPR course offered at a future date at your company, school, or Tora. Once you have determined that your student is OK, have them sit by the side and keep an eye on them. If the student is a Junior, seek out his or her parents or make sure that they are told by you what has happened. Your sensei should speak to the parents as well. If there is a real emergency, use a phone and call 911. One person should clearly explain the situation and perform first aid and another person should be assigned to wait at the door for an ambulance. Use one or two other students to keep the rest of the students away so the first aider can do their job.

19) My student is telling me that they were taught the technique differently by another instructor and they are asking, " Which is the right way?"

I wish I could tell you that there was one way to do a technique or a kata and one way only but it just isn't so. Tora will have a lot of techniques that we can agree should be done in a certain way like stances and basics, for example but as you go higher in rank, you may find that even black belts are doing things slightly different from one another. As you go through your training, an instructor may look at your technique and recommend you do something differently to correct a difficulty you are having. They will generally tell you that this is a correction personal to you and that you should continue to teach the generic version.

Karate is a live art. The Japanese were very reluctant to put things to paper because once it was printed, the art could no longer grow or change. Imagine if we treated science the same way and once something was in print, it couldn't change! There is a tendency to look at a martial art book and hold tight to the writing and pictures and say this is the way it is. It is really a snapshot in time of that particular art and should be taken as such. If your student brings up the fact that you are teaching differently from someone else, acknowledge it and ask them to do it the way you are explaining it for now. At the end of the class, bring up the matter with your instructor and they will look at the technique. There are also advanced versions of techniques that will be taught but there is a progression and a beginner will start out with a different technique in order to get them to an advanced level later. You and your student should try and remain flexible enough to be able to accept a change and run with it at least for the time you are being asked to do a technique differently. In real life, nothing is going to look exactly like the picture and no situation is going to unfold exactly like it did in training. The superior martial artist and person adapts to the situation with an open and clear mind.

20) I'm OK with teaching a few students at a time but teaching the whole class is a different story, isn't it?

Not really. In some ways, it can be easier. I have had instructors come up to me and express that it was easier to teach the larger group because it wasn't as intense. It all depends on how you look at the situation. First off, this is a friendly crowd; this isn't like standing up in front of a group of strangers. The people standing in front of you know it will be their turn at one point to do what you are doing and so they will try their best to follow along and make you look and feel good as you do for other instructors. When you first go in front of the class, just do the usual routine that you have done countless times as a student. To make you feel more comfortable, do what you are asking your students to do. There will already be some underlying respect for the position you are taking in front of the students but you can earn more respect for your character in general by working with them. When you ask them to stretch a bit harder, you do it to. When you ask them to run and do the push-ups and sit-ups, do it right alongside them. As you go higher in rank, you may not have to do everything in front of them but for now, it sets a good example and also gets rid of some of your own anxiety as the exercises will come automatically to you.

Use your outdoor voice for speaking and use your karate breathing with your stomach to project your words. When going through the warm-up, pick a person to watch that you know is of average fitness. Watch for when they are getting tired. If you build your warm-up around the most in shape person, the others might keel over before you have finished! One of the reasons you will be called up to do the warm-up is that it is fun to have some variety. Everyone has their strengths and this is where you can give part of yourself back to the club and teach them an exercise that you are good at. If you forget a part of the warm-up, just continue or add something different. We will generally take about fifteen to twenty minutes before we break up the class into groups.

21) I made it through the warm-up, now everyone is wondering what's next?

Now it's time split the class into smaller groups. There are going to be times when we keep the group together but when we have a large spread of ranks, this is one of the most effective ways to make sure everyone goes home with something new to work on. Don't be intimidated by the size of the group, just remember that each rank should be able to teach the ranks below them. Here is where you get to learn a bit of management. Each of the ranks has a certain capability. A lower rank should only be asked to teach a few students at a time so that they can easily focus their attention on them. A higher rank may be able to take a larger quantity of lower ranked students as the techniques will be more basic and require more repetition. Each class brings different people so there is generally no set rule about sectioning the class. Your sensei may also help in splitting the class if he or she has a goal for the evening. Even though you may feel a bit awkward doing so, it is ok for you to assign teaching to a higher rank. For example, if you are an orange belt in front of the class on that occasion, you may ask a brown belt to teach the blues and you can ask the browns to decide what to teach.

As instructors become more proficient and higher in rank, more responsibility and leeway will be given to them as to what to teach. It is part of the training to also learn to evaluate a student you have been given and chose a technique that needs to be taught. Black Belts don't become teachers overnight! Another dimension of splitting the class may look at individual capabilities. Tora has always had a wide variety of people attending the club and each may have a special strength or talent that could benefit the group or individuals. Here is a simple example; you are breaking up the class and you see you have a very tall and thin brown belt. Somewhere in the ranks is a teen that has just shot up in height like a bamboo shoot. This student is looking and feeling awkward in the new size body. It might be a good idea to get the tall brown belt to teach this student as they have already solved many of the movement problems that the teen is running into. Sometimes you may want to group by personality. You may see an instructor that exudes energy and you could ask this instructor work with some students that could shine if they could pull just a bit more energy from themselves. Getting to know your fellow students will help both your karate and in recognizing character traits and personalities. This leadership skill can be carried over to school or company organizations. As is the case with anything, the more you stand in front of the class, the easier it will become. Will you ever feel completely at ease? Probably not and maybe you should always have just enough sense of the unknown so that you try your best but you will be able to deal with it.

Karate, like other disciplines, is a way of life.

www.ingramcontent.com/pod-product-compliance
Lightning Source LLC
Chambersburg PA
CBHW070950040426
42443CB00012B/3289